After the Nightmare

Wendy Ovaris

LP LEARNING PUBLICATIONS, INC.
Holmes Beach, Florida

ISBN 1-55691-041-X

Learning Publications, Inc.
5351 Gulf Drive
P.O. Box 1338
Holmes Beach, FL 34218-1338

Printing: 6 5 4 3 2   Year: 7 6 5 4 3

Printed in the United States of America.

Dedication

To my son, Travis, who has taught me that the bond between mother and child, once established, can survive any challenge that life brings.

94670

Contents

Acknowledgements

My gratitude and respect for the women and children who have shared their experiences with me continues to grow daily. In addition I would like to thank Maureen Surgenor for her friendship and help in preparing the original manuscript, Geri Brooks for her wise counsel, Elizabeth Kubler-Ross for giving us a vehicle for understanding our grief, Jim McConnell for his help and support during the research phase of the project, and Edsel Erickson for believing I had something to share and making that possible.

1
INTRODUCTION

There is little in the literature for therapists that serves non-offending mothers in families where father-child incest occurs. That is the reason for this book. We have a recent but fast growing body of work from therapists who are now working with these mothers. These therapists bring to bear a heritage of practice and research on the mental health of mothers in families where there is incest. It is time that this work is shared.

This work must be shared because there still are too many myths — even among professionals — about the mother in father/child incest situations. Among these myths are that these mothers:

- knew about the incest and refused to do anything about it;

- were indifferent or absent;

- encouraged their children into incestuous relationships with father or stepfather;

- wanted their children to "mother" their spouses;

- were weak and submissive;

- kept themselves tired and worn out;

- were frigid; and

- wanted to reverse roles with their daughters.

As McIntyre (1980) pointed out over a decade ago, the message to mothers is clear: they are seen as directly or indirectly contributing to the incest. This false assumption has led to three myths: (1) the incestuous father is "victim" of the mother's weakness; (2) the incestuous father is a person who is simply confused about his responsibilities as a father; and (3) treatment should focus exclusively on the mother. As will be elaborated upon in a later discussion, these views are absurd.

These stereotypes, shared by professionals and the general public, provide offenders with a ready supply of justifications for their inappropriate conduct. In my experience it is not uncommon for fathers or father surrogates to use the inadequacies of their spouse to justify assaulting their children. We must always remember that the offender is responsible for his behavior. And as therapists, we must be conscious of not reinforcing the projections he has already imposed on his non-offending spouse and child.

My purpose is to present insights into the experiences of non-offending mothers when their children have been sexually abused. The sources of my information are primarily the women and children who have shared their experiences of incest with me and allowed me to assist them as a crisis counselor and therapist.

I have learned that the first task of any therapist is to assume that the mother is not guilty of causing the abuse. This working premise enhances dialogue in the therapeutic relationship and facilitates decision-making in the best interests of both parent and child.

My work with non-offending fathers has been limited. However, with them I have consistently encountered fears and defensiveness that they will be blamed for the assault of their child. These fathers typically deny the abuse or otherwise justify their conduct by relying on the stereotypes about mothers. With these fathers, debunking the myths is critical in order for therapists to help overcome the perpetrator's denial. When non-offending fathers no longer accept these myths as true, they are less likely to blame their spouses. This in turn helps in the mother's recovery.

As professionals, we should understand how our beliefs shape our therapy. We have to know when we are responding according to a false assumption and when we are dealing with the truth. We have to be clear about whether we seek understanding for the purpose of finding out who is to blame for the problem, or for the purpose of helping our client. Anyone I know who has worked with incest has had to undergo some process of self-awareness. This is best done through a fellow therapist, supervisor or colleague — not a client.

To further complicate matters, there are many false beliefs about parenting which contribute to a parent's guilt and shock when their child has been hurt. Some of the myths that most therapists recognize are reflected in the following statements:

- "Mothers have total responsibility for everything that happens to her child."

- "Mothers should always know what to do."

- "*Good* mothers have happy, healthy children."

- "Mothers must not let their children see that they are scared or vulnerable."

- "If parents cannot (or do not) control their child's life, they are incompetent."

- "If mothers are around (i.e., alive), no harm can come to their child."

- "If mothers really love their children, they can protect them from anything."

- "A child's well-being is proof of a mother's love for him or her."

This cluster of myths suggests that we must be cautious in developing generalizations about mothers in incestuous families. The responses and circumstances of mothers will vary with the uniqueness of their own personalities, needs and life experiences.

What follows is a description of the variety of experiences I have observed and shared with non-offending mothers of children who were sexually abused by someone in their families. Suggestions will be offered which, hopefully, will help therapists in assisting these mothers to deal with the aftermath of their child's sexual abuse. My hope is to increase sensitivity and understanding regarding non-offending mothers while enhancing the quality of services available to them.

2

THE NON-OFFENDING MOTHER'S PERSONAL EXPERIENCE

Contrary to assertions about the characteristics of mothers of sexually abused children, I do not believe that anyone can provide a reliable or valid profile of them or their children. A serious oversight in attempts to identify causality or precipitating factors in child sexual abuse is that we do not know very much about the mothers of victims until after the abuse has been disclosed.

Analysis of the mother's personality type or behavioral characteristics usually is conducted under extreme stress. It is therefore important not to confuse her stress responses with how she behaved in her family while the incest was occurring. Within the context of the crisis, all parties involved will be struggling to understand why this tragedy occurred. Unfortunately, the temptation to "know" why it happened can override the objective of gathering more information and understanding the uniqueness, needs and circumstances of the individuals involved.

Once we impose a judgement on a non-offending mother, we make decisions about what she needs and what she will do. We try to make her fit our understanding and abilities. However, if we approach her with the understanding that we know only some of what she is experiencing, we are more likely to gather the information required to make informed decisions.

The mothers I have encountered are diverse in their personalities, backgrounds and socioeconomic status. It is a mistake to assume that their needs and responses will be identical. Nevertheless, there are common elements which set non-offending mothers apart. What differentiates them from many parents not experiencing a personal crisis (such as that imposed by the recognition of incest) are the behaviors or "symptoms" they experience as a consequence of extreme stress.

3
THE CRISIS OF DISCLOSURE

The crisis for a non-offending mother begins with the disclosure or discovery of the abuse. Regrettably, judgments that she "should" have known or "could" have known function to blame her for circumstances beyond her control. How and when recognition takes place will vary significantly. Three factors must be given serious consideration:

1. Child sexual abuse, especially incest, is a matter of tremendous secrecy. Perpetrators invest a great deal of energy in ensuring that they are not discovered; they will press their children into secrecy through any means available or effective.

2. No mother *wants* to believe her child is being harmed, especially by someone with whom both she and her child have a dependent, close and caring relationship. Most mothers

will exhaust a broad range of possible causes for their child's problems before considering sources close to home.

3. In confronting their child's crisis, the mother enters a personal crisis which will challenge all her inner and external resources. The resources available for such a crisis vary significantly with each individual. Few human beings enter a personal crisis of the intensity of incest consciously and willingly. The self-protective stances of denial or avoidance in most crisis situations are natural.

In focusing on the well-being of the child and on punishment of the offender, it is easy to ignore the personal crisis being experienced by the non-offending mother. Unfortunately, many police, social workers, teachers and others have an implicit expectation that mothers in an incestuous situation will immediately accept disclosure of the incest as an unequivocal truth. It is also assumed that these mothers will take whatever action professionals recommend to them. Neither assumption is necessarily true.

Consider the following experience. A mother is in her mid-thirties, she is a nurse working part-time, has three children (ages 9, 6, and 11) and has been married for 13 years. She has worked consistently during her marriage to enhance her family's lifestyle. Her marriage isn't perfect, but appears to be stable. One afternoon a social worker and a policeman appear at her door and ask to see her husband. She explains he won't be home for an hour and asks what they want. They come in, sit down and say they will wait for her husband to return. Her anxiety is rising and her assumptions are racing. They tell her that her nine year old daughter told her teacher that her dad was "touching her in bad places and she was scared." A social worker interviewed the child and thought the evidence warranted an investigation.

What would be the expected response of a mother to such an encounter? An enthusiastic or calm acceptance of the information as true? A spontaneous affirmation that her husband could be molesting his own child? Immediate validation of her daughter's *alleged* statements about her father? The answer to all of these questions is "no."

In our society loyalty is valued in family relationships. Loyalty is understood to mean supporting and trusting a person in periods of adversity. With incest, the mother finds herself in a serious psychological, emotional and moral dilemma. She is being called upon to be loyal to one family member (her child) and withdraw her support from another (her husband). If the marriage is still intact, regardless of its dynamics, the mother will likely show some semblance of commitment or responsibility toward her husband.

Further, her dilemma will be apparent in her reaction to the disclosure. Most likely the mother will not want to believe that the incest has taken place. This is too often interpreted as her "refusing to believe the truth" or that she is deserting her child. It is also important to remember that a mother's denials and doubts are likely to be reinforced by the persistent denials of her husband. Statements like "It can't be true," "Why would she say something like this?" "She's destroying our family," can be taken out of context and incorrectly interpreted as not caring for or having a commitment to her child.

The mother who finds out that her child has been sexually abused will be confused, angry, frightened and hurt. It is essential that the emotions underlying the behavior and statements of mothers in such situations be taken into account. They are experiencing *personal* crises, apart from their children or spouses, and apart from their roles as wives and mothers. The temptation to use their reaction to disclosure as a basis for understanding their role as mothers, or the family dynamics, must be resisted. Negative judgments of mothers who *appear* to reject their children or to deny disclosure will alienate them from those who can help them. They will probably adopt defenses which hinder communication with them. They are likely to feel pressured to "take a stand" while in a highly confused and stressed state.

Similarly, premature judgments of a mother who immediately rallies to take action on behalf of her child, may overlook that she may be in shock and will need support. Guilt is an inevitable maternal response to assertions of child abuse. A mother who, in this crisis state, receives all her affirmations for being strong by "getting rid of that bastard" and "protecting her child," will be hesitant to admit her own fears and confusion. She will try to conceal them from others and from herself. This can block the grieving process and inhibit her ability to confront painful issues which emerge after the initial crisis. It is suggested that such mothers not be subtly or overtly forced into "confessing" underlying fears. Rather, we should seek to understand that hers is a stress response.

We must understand that each woman's reaction to the crisis incest presents will vary according to her personal characteristics and resources, especially her self-esteem. Her self-esteem will affect and be affected by:

1. What she believes are her alternatives in the situation;

2. How she perceives her relationship with the child and with the offender;

3. What fears and losses she faces;

4. What meaning she gives to the situation; and

5. How she responds to therapeutic interventions.

These forces will become more apparent as the crisis evolves. However, they are triggered at the point the crisis is acknowledged.

The mother's response will also be affected by the nature of the offender's relationship to the child. It is generally accepted by professionals working in this area that incest results in a more intense trauma for child victims, as compared to extra-familial or stranger assaults. This has been attributed to:

1. The power of the offender in the child's life;

2. The intimate relationship between the child and offender;

3. The duration of the abuse; and

4. The violation of bonds of trust and protection associated with being a parent.

In addition, it has been my experience that the following factors have a significant impact on the responses of non-offending mothers:

1. The power of the offender in the mother's life;

2. The character of the intimate relationship between the mother and the offender;

3. The duration of the abuse; and

4. The violation of trust.

The woman who feels powerless in her relationship with the offender (e.g., her husband) will respond to disclosure of the abuse with a proportionate sense of powerlessness. A woman will probably be less willing to accept her husband being a child molester than if the molester is a distant relative. A mother's guilt, and consequent defensive reactions, will be intensified if the abuse continued over a long period of time and she did not know about it.

In circumstances where the biological father does not reside with mother and child, and the alleged offender is a step or live-in father figure, special complications can arise. The character and intensity of these will be influenced significantly by the quality of the relationship between the estranged parents. Both will be experiencing guilt and distress, and they will be tempted to project blame and demands for a solution onto one another.

The non-custodial biological father may initiate or renew efforts to gain custody of his child. The mother may choose to resist or cooperate, depending on her own circumstances and confidence in her ability to protect her child. It is important that involved professionals be able to separate the issues in the relationship between estranged parents and those precipitated by the incest situation.

Decisions regarding long-term custody or a radical change in the child's living arrangements should not be made in the immediacy of the crisis, unless it is clear the child's welfare is at stake. Parents should be encouraged to separate personal differences from concerns for their child. Whenever possible the therapeutic goal is to help parents work together toward the best interests of their child. A child's trauma will be intensified if she or he becomes a pawn in a power struggle.

Remember that disclosure represents the beginning of the crisis for non-offending mothers. Hopefully, disclosure also represents the conclusion of the incest and the beginning of the healing process for the child. However, as stated, the tendency of many concerned professionals and other adults is to assume that the non-offending mother will immediately respond as a competent and cooperative "colleague," focusing all of her energy and attention on the well-being of her child. It is important to recognize that she may not have the immediate resources necessary to do this. It is also important to remember that mothers need time and support for their healing to occur.

4
THE GRIEVING PROCESS FOR NON-OFFENDING MOTHERS

The Elizabeth Kubler-Ross *grief cycle* provides a model for the process I have witnessed among women whose children have been sexually abused:

1. Stage One: denial

2. Stage Two: anger

3. Stage Three: bargaining

4. Stage Four: depression

5. Stage Five: acceptance

By understanding a mother's experience as a series of stages, the risk of either a "helper" or mother getting stuck at any one stage is reduced. Identifying this process to mothers can reduce fears that their initial feelings are all that is to come "forever after." This is important to their understanding of their child's reactions as well.

Stage One: Denial

"It can't be real," is not an uncommon statement from parents who discover that their child has been seriously harmed or abused. There is an element of "naturalness" in not wanting to believe that an act considered horrendous in our society has been committed by, or against, a loved one. Allowing a mother time to assimilate what has taken place will be more important and effective than pressuring her to "admit" that the abuse has taken place.

The mother's denial is likely to be expressed in several possible ways including:

- denial that incest took place,

- accepting that incest took place but denying that it was harmful to the child, and

- denial that she, the offender, and the child need any "outside" intervention from protective services.

A mother who brings a reasonable level of self-awareness and ego strength into a crisis (i.e., has some understanding and acceptance of her own emotional and psychological responses) can gain solace from understanding that she is in a state of denial.

Entering the grief process, the non-offending mother faces losses of varying character and intensity. These losses are painful and avoidance is a typical response. The losses confronting the mother will likely include:

- the "lost innocence" of the child and that of siblings;

- loss of a sense of safety in the world;

- lost social life;

- lost friends and family members who will not accept the situation, or blame her in some way for its occurrence;

- diminished self-confidence;

- loss of a spouse;

- loss of a parenting partner;

- loss of self-image as a "good" parent;

- lost income;

- diminished freedom; and

- lost home.

For some mothers, fear of such losses is a compelling aspect of their denial and of certain dysfunctional behaviors. Included here is the mother who tries to explain away her husband's behavior as totally out of character and *never* happening again (e.g., "he was drunk," "she seduced him," "he's been under so much stress he doesn't know what he's doing"). In this case, her fear of losing her husband and the security he represents assumes greater priority than protecting her daughter from future abuse.

Professionals should be sensitive to the non-offending mother as an individual, apart from her responsibilities as a mother. In the example given, the approach could be to "speak to" her fear rather than try to convince her that incest is rarely a situational occurrence (e.g., "It is hard to accept that your husband molested your own daughter. What he's done can mean changes in your life that seem overwhelming right now.").

Other examples of a mother resisting confronting possible losses include:

- minimizing the child's trauma;

- focusing on her husband changing other behaviors (e.g., stop drinking);

- clinging to therapy as a guaranteed solution to his problems; or

- blaming herself in accordance with the stereotypes and myths mentioned earlier.

The intensity of a non-offending mother's denial cannot discount the safety needs of the child or children. If it is determined that children are indeed at risk and the mother will not cooperate by separating them from the offender, some action by government agencies might have to be taken (i.e., taking the children into temporary custody, ordering the offender out of the home, or insisting that the mother leave with the children). However, such action can be undertaken with compassion and without judging her to be inadequate or an "accomplice."

Empathy is likely to be the most effective strategy for engaging a mother in the denial stage. Professionals can suggest that the mother seek child care in order to take time to focus on her own adjustment needs. She should be encouraged to talk about what she *is* feeling, rather than what she *should* be feeling. Informed of what steps will be taken in an investigation of incest, or treatment of the child, she can be reassured that no radical actions or decisions will take place without her involvement.

It is important to mention that denial may re-emerge as a response to new circumstances and information. This is not considered regression; it is normal as both mother and child work through their concerns and changes in the circumstances imposed on them.

Stage Two: Anger

A mother's realization and acceptance that incest has taken place can produce anger toward her child, the offender or herself. This anger is closely related to seeking a reason for why the abuse occurred. The person she identifies as *causing* the abuse will likely be the focus of her anger. This can be the child, the offender, or possibly even herself. In addition, a non-offending mother's anger can change frequently. This reflects her feelings of betrayal, powerlessness, guilt, hurt, and a hopelessness that what has happened cannot be undone.

Mothers need to learn a simple truism about incest: a definitive answer for *why* any child has been victimized is not possible. The closest we are ever able to come, with retroactive assessments, is on probable factors that might have been involved. In the overwhelming majority of cases, these factors could not have been seen or controlled by mothers before the fact.

If properly channeled, however, anger can be a valuable tool in her recovery. The value of her anger is as a catalyst to release feelings and to help illuminate the forces underlying them. Where this can be done constructively, her anger is less likely to be projected onto the child. With support, these mothers will cease to blame themselves or their children.

Mothers can effectively process their anger in a variety of ways. Keeping a personal journal provides a medium for expressing thoughts and feelings, as well as a record of emerging memories or observations which can be shared with supportive professionals. Physical activities, such as exercise or walking, also can help. Similarly, deep breathing exercises can induce calm and help center the individual. Mothers will need support in exploring a variety of strategies for releasing feelings in a manner that is comfortable, constructive and easy to access.

When outsiders focus too much on protecting the child, they often fail to check out a mother's support network working through her grief. Lacking support, a tremendous strain is placed on a woman's self-esteem. The anger she feels can emerge and express itself in a variety of ways including:

- fear of acknowledging or expressing her anger toward the offender because of his perceived power in a her life;

- overwhelming depression or anger toward herself;

- reacting to the child's anger, which can often be projected onto the non-offending parent as being responsible for the changes which follow disclosure of the abuse;

- a stress response; or

- a frantic search for "why."

When a mother accepts her anger as legitimate, she is less likely to act out inappropriately.

Guilt is a form of anger directed toward one's self; it can be as emotionally and psychologically draining as anger directed outward. The key point is what a mother does with her anger and not that she feels anger.

I have found it futile to simply reassure a mother that she is not the guilty party in her child's abuse. Once again, empathy appears to be the most effective intervention. One should help the mother to review her circumstances for a more objective assessment of what she can or could reasonably control. I have found it effective to recount the situation in the third person (e.g., "If I told you about a woman who ..." and conclude with "... and what would your judgement of her be?"). Such an approach takes the women into a more accepting stance. It is important not to absolve mothers of their responsibilities, but rather to bring their expectations and judgments into a realistic perspective.

There will be mothers who are so threatened by, or dependent upon, the offender (e.g., a husband) that they are unable to divert or explore the source of their anger. This can cause serious problems. For example, if a non-offending mother directs anger toward her child, the child's safety and well-being have to be taken into account.

Anger toward an offender is the response we usually expect and accept. However, in father-child incest, this anger is not separated from a mother's grief, hurt, and feelings toward her husband. One moment she may be making charges and demanding that police take him out of the home. Later she may want to drop charges because "He promises he'll never do it again;" "The children need their father;" "I can't help it, I can't stop loving the man." These reactions are understandable in light of the complexity of the problem.

Often professionals are anxious when a woman appears to be diverting from action they perceive as correct or essential. Suggesting to her that many women in similar circumstances experience this confusion will reduce her defensiveness by giving legitimacy to her feelings. My experience is that most women are willing to cooperate in therapy once they trust that they are not being criticized or labelled for their confusion.

Anger toward the offender can also be expressed as a desire for revenge. She may wish to take the law into her own hands. She may place unrealistic demands on the criminal justice system to take action. She may even use her children as a tool to get revenge against her husband. Such responses are inappropriate because they tend to make her situation worse, and they may place the children at further risk. Anger directed into revenge is not therapeutic.

The mother must be assisted in realizing that her anger can be expressed in ways less threatening to her and to her children's future. Neither dismiss an angry mother's threats of violence, nor treat her threats as inevitable. The anger itself must be recognized and respected, and the possible consequences of these threats explored. Once a mother lets go of the possibility of "eliminating" the offender from her life completely, she usually moves into the experience of pain and despair underlying the anger.

Moreover, a mother's dependence on the criminal justice system to "justly punish" her husband and prove his guilt can be an unrealistic expectation. We are still struggling with police and court procedures in child sexual abuse, and it is difficult for the lay person to understand why an apparently "known" offender can avoid punishment because of legal technicalities. Helping a mother understand what a conviction and severe sentence mean to her (i.e., what needs and concerns the conviction may or may not resolve) can help her in ways other than depending on the outcome in court.

A non-offending mother will usually interpret her husband's conviction as further evidence:

- of his guilt;

- of her child's innocence;

- of her own innocence;

- that her child and other children will be protected from him;

- that she could not have protected her child any better than she did from someone as "sick" as her husband;

- that he will suffer for what he did; and

- that she took "right action" and protected her child and society by taking him to court.

However, a conviction will not necessarily result in relief from all anger. Anger will continue to be experienced at each stage in the mother's and child's healing process.

Stage Three: Bargaining

Bargaining is the stage where we hear a mother making statements which demand or expect a complete resolution of her trauma and that of her child. She will want to know if therapy will *really* work. She will express an urgent desire for direction on what she can do to "make it all right." She may cling to information or statements from others that say sexual abuse does not *really* hurt children, or that lots of men only do it *once*. The theme in this stage is "what can I do to make it all go away?" The painful reality is that the answer to this question is: "Nothing will make it all go away."

In coming to terms with her anger, she may appear ready to try and heal herself and her child. However, she should be aided not to overestimate her capabilities. Giving her direction in parenting her traumatized child, without checking out her support network or resources, can contribute to even more stress. She is searching for a "magic fix-it," and if this goal is not achieved, she may judge herself as the cause of that failure. This further damages her already eroded self-esteem, and depletes the energy available for her own recovery.

Provide feedback and support which will keep a mother's expectations of herself and her child within realistic limits. Encourage her to take small steps; this will help prepare her for successes rather than failures.

It is essential to keep a mother clearly informed and involved with regard to every action and decision being taken on her or her family's behalf. This reinforces her confidence and sense of control as an individual and a

parent.   It also diminishes potentially unrealistic
expectations of "experts."

   In wanting everything "all better," most mothers
desire to have circumstances return to the status quo.
From this perspective, any differences or changes in
their child can be seen as failures or proof of inadequacy.
Responsibilities for this may be placed with intervening
professionals, themselves, the "system," their husband's
continued interference, or anyone else involved — even
God. In this situation, a mother needs help in realizing
that life can never go back to the way it was. Changes in
the child or in circumstances should be presented
realistically. For example:

- a child's acting out can be seen as an expression
  of feelings that need to be expressed;

- the action taken by a mother after she discovers
  the sexual abuse can be portrayed as helping to
  rebuild a child's trust and sense of safety; and

- the mother's confronting of her husband's
  molesting behavior can be seen as healthy in that
  it serves to protect children and to create an
  opportunity for the family to receive needed help.

The above examples do not discount the pain or the seriousness of sexual abuse, but hopefully will show that even in tragedy, some gains are possible.

In a desire for life to be as it was before the abuse was discovered, a non-offending mother may try to "normalize" her husband's behaviors. This may take the form of her believing that:

- his promises to never do it again are valid;

- he is a good father is every other way;

- if he stops drinking, there would be no problem;

- the impact of the incest on her child wasn't serious ("he *just* touched her"); and

- the daughter was responsible for the abuse or "I really *wasn't* a good wife."

This bargaining with self and others reflects the fears a mother wants to resolve or avoid. If such bargaining revolves around her husband, she can say that he is what she most fears losing. If it revolves around her child's recovery, and her husband is "out of the picture," the mother may express fears about the long term consequences for her child. If it revolves around her husband's qualities and importance as a parent, she may express fears about her own competence or about the possibility of single parenthood. The important point is to identify and address those fears contributing to her attempts to bargain.

A mother who clings to false expectations cannot be coerced into accepting the "truth." However, her need to believe in false expectations can be respected and responded to gently and with sensitivity.

Stage Four: Depression and Withdrawal

As the mother gradually recognizes that the situation will not go away, she may appear to give up hope that things will ever get better. Her child's anger, anxiety, bedwetting or nightmares may increase. Exhausted by the process of dealing with her child's problems through engaging social or psychological services, she may become apathetic. She may feel too tired to try anything else to solve her problems.

However, at the same time a mother of an incest victim appears to be giving up all hope, she may actually be starting to accept the reality of her experiences and the changes ahead of her. It is important not to try and explain away her despair, but rather allow her to explore and express her feelings of exhaustion. In the previous stages, her energy was involved in repression or projection. In this stage she opens up to her need for renewal and energy. Allowed to withdraw and "recharge," she is likely to see positive potentials for change.

Arguing with her about her sense of hopelessness can further deplete her energy and make her feel vulnerable. This vulnerability, however, may cause her to reject her own preferences and capabilities. The task of the therapist is to place the mother in the position of mobilizing her own resources for recovery.   It is therefore important to keep the mother involved in any decisions regarding her or her family, and at the same time remain sensitive to the resources she has available to invest in the tasks at hand.

There may be friends, family members and possibly even professionals who refuse to believe that the abuse has occurred. These individuals may withdraw support. When people withdraw their support, the mothers interpret this as "all is lost," because "no one cares." They think "what is the point of trying?" Non-offending mothers are vulnerable to criticism and judgments from others.

Judgments that she is uncaring, weak, paranoid or unmotivated, have been experienced by most of these mothers. In addition, mothers may impose these judgments on themselves, further fueling their depression.

The task of the therapist is twofold. First, the therapist should help a non-offending mother to understand these experiences as normal. This will help her to gain perspective and to realize that she is not "going crazy." Second, the therapist should help a mother to identify all of the resources for recovery at her disposal so that she does not feel overwhelmed. The ultimate goal is to help her regain her sense of competence and autonomy. Simply stated, she needs to be put into a position where she can regain a sense of control over her life.

The intensity and character of a mother's feelings of depression should be monitored carefully. Her psychological history, previous stress responses, and self-esteem will influence how she copes. A woman who has previously considered suicide may do so again in this situation. Her importance to her children's welfare and her ability to overcome present challenges must be consistently reinforced.

Extreme withdrawal or apathy in a mother's behavior should be viewed in the context of her children's well-being and safety. Child care and housekeeping support may be important for her.

I recommend against separating mothers and children during this stage, because of the risk of ratifying a mother's belief in her own incompetence and worthlessness to her children. Short-term and well-monitored medical interventions (e.g., anti-depressants) may help in some cases. The point is to continue moving her through the grief experience to a point of resolution.

Helping her to regain a sense of control is critical with respect to one of the most important decisions she will have to make. She will have to decide what to do about her marriage. There is no truth in the assertion that an incest offender never can be rehabilitated, or that no marriage can survive the trauma of incest. However, a woman who chooses to maintain a relationship with her spouse who has committed incest should do so with "her eyes open." She should recognize the potential risks as well as the benefits in order to make an informed decision. Some of the concerns that must be taken into account are the:

- safety and well-being of the children during the period of the father's efforts to change;

- mother's recognition of all the things necessary for her security in the relationship;

- knowledge that no therapy can guarantee results;

- recognition that the fathers are also under duress and are likely to make promises that they will not necessarily keep;

- understanding that what has happened cannot be ignored or taken back;

- realization that all family members will be changed because of the incest;

- self-esteem and ego strength of the father may not be adequate to withstand the stress of new demands on him as he seeks re-entry into the family;

- mother's avoidance of fearful situations will not resolve her problems with her husband;

- mother and child are not likely to feel more secure and confident in the relationship than previously.

A woman choosing to reconcile with her husband should be aware of these concerns. If reconciliation seems likely, the needs of the children should be evaluated and appropriate action taken by relevant agencies if necessary.

On the other hand, therapists should also remember that a mother's depression and withdrawal may result in her isolating herself and her child(ren) from the rest of her family, friends, and other potential support. Referring to her attempts at isolation as "silly" or "over protective," and insisting that she "get on with her life," will only alienate her further. This stage, like the others, must be experienced before it can be resolved. Like the others, it too may be re-experienced. But with help, a mother of an incest victim can come to understand that her misery will not last. If anything, her feelings of helplessness and her desire to surrender are temporary; they are signals that life may get better.

Stage Five: Acceptance

The final stage, acceptance, is when the mother realizes that each obstacle she faces no longer prophesizes permanent suffering. During this stage, the non-offending mother recognizes that the incest has taken place; that circumstances and people have changed and that they will continue to change. The mother's

expectations of herself and her child are reasonably
realistic in that they are seen as achievable. Her
struggles are less frantic or urgent.

During this stage, the incest is no longer the focus
of every action. The mother will seem more relaxed in
letting her child out into the world and allowing others to
be involved with her and her child. The result is that the
reactions of others seem less threatening to her. She is
likely to become more involved and assertive in services
provided to her child and should be less defensive or
anxious about suggestions, recommendations or
assessments.

A mother able to reach this stage of acceptance will
have more patience and confidence in her child's
recovery. Having experienced a process of healing
herself, she will have more confidence in this possibility
for her child. She will also be able to model for her child
the healthy behaviors common to those who have
overcome a serious trauma. At this point, for mother
and child, the victims become survivors.

5
EMOTIONAL AND PSYCHOLOGICAL CONSEQUENCES FOR THE MOTHER

The emotional and psychological patterns experienced by non-offending mothers are not significantly different than those seen in primary victims. This includes:

- guilt;

- generalized fear;

- grief and loss;

- powerlessness;

- self-esteem issues.

Guilt

It is common for nearly all non-offending mothers to say "I should have known." No matter at what point she realizes that her child has been sexually abused, she will think of something that should have been a clue to her realizing what was happening. This causes guilt. However, she should learn that even if she had recognized a clue, the incest may have occurred. Further, there are no single clues which inevitably forecast incest. Finally, she needs to understand that even if certain clues were present, the mother is never responsible for the actions of the offender.

The mother's feelings of guilt may be influenced by the child's age, the duration of the sexual abuse, and symptoms in the child which preceded the disclosure or discovery of the abuse. We view infants and young children as more vulnerable and, therefore, in need of greater protection by caregivers. Mothers of young incest victims tend to chastise themselves intensely for not protecting their offspring. At the same time, these children are less critical of parental behavior, less able to assess or identify an assault and less likely to expose an offending parent. Symptoms of sexual abuse (e.g., anxiety, bedwetting, genital irritation, nightmares, etc.) are only conclusive when viewed collectively. Individually these symptoms may seem to be normal childhood ailments. In the discovery of incest with very young children, mothers need to be supported through the difficulty of this assessment and congratulated for the action they did take on their child's behalf.

Incest disclosed by an adolescent most likely has taken place over an extended period of time. Older children are more inclined to take responsibility for the sexual abuse themselves, and their decision to keep the incest secret includes protecting their own shame as well as any threats imposed by the perpetrator. Mothers of these children may blame the child for not disclosing earlier, for being a willing accomplice, or for trying to create trouble for a disliked parent or other family members.

Often in discussing incest with a teenager, therapists forget that the victim most likely was very young when the incest began. Both mothers and victims need to be reminded of this fact. Adolescents are also more likely than young children to assume that a mother should or did have some knowledge of what was going on. Incestuous fathers are known to discuss their spouse's sexual inadequacies with their older incest victims, implying this as the cause of their own behaviors. These dynamics can reinforce maternal guilt or a "blame exchange" between mother and child.

Both mother and child need to be reminded that every time they blame themselves or one another for the incest, they are absolving the offender of his responsibility. Family therapy can provide a sensitive and supportive context for sorting out the pieces of the incest puzzle.

Sexually abusive adults go to great effort to ensure that their behavior is kept secret. The closer their relationship with the victim, the more successful they are in keeping the sexual abuse secret. However, if a mother learns that incest has occurred, she may believe that she should have been "all knowing" of any dangers to her children. The important point to bring to the attention of the mother is that unless she participated in the assault, or actively and consciously encouraged it, she is not responsible for the sexual abuse of her child.

Feelings of guilt at not knowing the dangers their children are facing is a special problem for mothers who themselves were abused as children. These mothers will feel "Of all people, I should have realized because it also happened to me." Not only will her guilt be intensified, but her child's victimization may cause a host of unresolved issues from the mother's past to re-emerge. The therapist is now confronted with dealing with a past crisis, as well as the present one.

Nevertheless, therapists should avoid elevating the non-offending mother to sainthood, ascribing all problems past and present to the offender. I believe that the mother has to gain perspective based on what she has done or not done. A technique I have found to be useful is to ask the mother the following questions:

- What did she do when she thought that something was wrong with her child?

- What did she do when she found out about the abuse?

- Why did she responded that way?

- What could she have done differently *with what she knew at any given time* to prevent the abuse?

It has also been effective for me to say to a mother, "If I told you about a woman who ... ," then recount her story back to her and ask what judgement she would make of this person. This usually helps her to look at these kind of responses in an objective manner.

It is important to encourage a mother to describe what she believes are her past mistakes. Then help her restate these errors in more positive terms. Ask the mother what she has learned from her experience and how she can invest that knowledge constructively. In doing this a supportive, non-judgmental approach is essential.

Generalized Fear

Discovering that the world is not a safe place for a loved one or oneself can result in a generalized fear of one's environment. One experience of a mother who recognizes that her husband has committed incest is usually that he made not only her child's life unsafe, but hers too. The father, in his position of trust and responsibility, has seriously violated the safety of both mother and child. The more the mother values her child and husband, the more unsafe she is likely to feel.

For those involved in the investigation or treatment of sexual abuse cases, it is important to recognize that both mother and child will have fears. They will be suspicious of anyone expecting them to disclose what they know. A mother should not be quickly labelled as "uncooperative" or "secretive" when in fact she is simply afraid of what has happened or may happen. Fear of being judged will usually cause both mother and victim to withdraw. They also may become antagonistic toward those seeking to help them.

Because many mothers will find it difficult to believe that their child has been sexually assaulted, they will be very sensitive to comments or questions such as: "How do you know?" or "Where were you when it happened?" or "What proof do you have that your child was not lying?" Remember, the role of the therapist is not to interrogate the mother but to put her in a position where she has greater understanding and control over her life.

Mothers need time to recover from the shock. They cannot be expected to instantly understand and accept the investigation process, as well as the complex responses of family, friends or others. Patience and clear explanations of the purpose of each intervention can help a mother work through her fears.

It is also common among mothers to fear that they or their children will be labelled "damaged goods." Among the mothers of abused boys, there exists a pervasive fear that their sons will be homosexual as a consequence of being victimized. Similarly, mothers of daughters fear that the child's sexual development may result in lesbianism or promiscuity. There are several ideas that the mother should be helped to accept:

- No one has the ability to accurately predict the long term consequences of sexual abuse;

- There is a lot of myth regarding sexual behaviors that are seen as deviant or dysfunctional;

- There is great risk of attributing all problems or struggles that an abused child will experience to the sexual abuse. Children who have not been abused often have some of the same problems as sexually abused children;

- Most victims can and do recover.

The process of resolving generalized fears will be long-term. Allowing a mother to discuss them openly as they emerge, is probably the most effective action we can take. Again, providing a woman with an opportunity to understand her experiences will enhance her ability to provide the same for her children.

Every interaction with a non-offending mother should strive to re-establish some sense of safety in her environment. However, her trust in her husband has been seriously violated. Thus, any experience that helps her trust another person will help her realize that every contact does not put her safety at risk. Therapists should provide her with exercises which will help her to regain a sense of trust in others. Then she will be able to realize that every relationship need not be characterized by betrayal.

Grief and Loss

Many unresolved problems for a non-offending mother will not emerge until a certain stimulus is encountered. Consider the case of a young mother of a four-year-old son who was assaulted by his father. When the abuse was discovered, the father immediately left home. For the next nine months, the mother's time and attention were taken up by court procedures, economic adjustments, adjusting to the lifestyle of a single parent, and treatment services for her son. Feeling lonely in a lifestyle dominated by work and children, she decided to begin dating. After the first encounter, she was confronted by the dilemma of wanting a relationship, and experiencing fear of intimacy with a man. It was at this point that she needed to understand the deeper implications of her anger toward her husband, and to grieve the loss of his companionship and partnership as a parent. The "good riddance to bad rubbish" reaction did not resolve her sense of betrayal and loss.

As a therapist, I initially found it difficult to understand the desire of mothers to have their children maintain contact with their abusive fathers. I had a particularly difficult time understanding this when there was no desire by the mother for reconciliation with her husband. Gradually I learned that mothers may want to protect their children from the complete loss of the other parent. In other words, despite the marriage being over, many mothers will maintain a relationship with offending fathers for the sake of the children.

This relationship, however, continues to be a source of anxiety for the mother. Therapists need to help non-offending mothers explore what it is about their relationship with the child's father they wanted to maintain. I learned to explore more fully why they want their child not to lose contact with their father, and how this could be accomplished in the best interests of their child. During this process, some mothers experienced fantasies of a positive relationship that they were trying to hang onto; others identified events that happened that they wanted to retain in memory. Some were able to communicate their desires to their children and in doing so, they became more proficient in listening to their children express their needs.

Sibling incest introduces another dynamic in the losses experienced by the parent. For example, one mother's initial reaction to the assault of both of her daughters by her teenage son was extreme anger at him. The boy was removed from the home, and both girls were placed in therapy. As the situation stabilized and the mother joined the girls in family therapy, she found herself defending her son when the girls expressed anger toward their brother. The pain in facing her son's disturbance, and the risk he presented for his sisters, brought to her awareness a tremendous sense of loss. After all, she remained his mother despite what he did to his sisters. The entire family dynamic had been altered, and the mother's loyalties were divided between the needs of her son and those of her daughters. In a very real sense, the protectiveness and responsibility that a mother shows for her child who is an offender is more intense than what she shows toward her husband.

This should not be surprising in view of the responsibility our society ascribes to parents for their children's behavior. Being the mother of a sexual offender is a difficult stigma to overcome. Treatment of the offender will inevitably bring to light problems and dysfunction in the offender's own childhood.

Often sexual abuse in the offender's background will be discovered. Whatever details emerge, inadequacies in the quality of parenting will probably be identified. This diverges critically from the mother's role in father-daughter incest, where the mother will not be assumed to have nearly as much influence or responsibility in the actions or motivation of the offender. The mother in sibling incest is in dire need of support which acknowledges that she is doing the best she can, and encourages her to focus on action and direction in the present.

Another dynamic in sibling incest is that we generally do not support parents "divorcing" their children. The offender may be removed from the home, charged as a young offender, and engaged in some form of treatment. It can be expected that contact with the family will be maintained or resumed. I believe family therapy is critical for the offender's relationship and re-entry in the family system. A family's adjustment in this situation should not be underestimated or unsupported. Mothers will need all the strength and confidence they can muster to achieve this adjustment.

I believe that it is unreasonable to press mothers to choose between their children when sibling incest is present. A mother is as potentially critical to the rehabilitation of an offender as to the recovery of the victim. Where she will benefit is in guidance and support in the different demands placed upon her in "being there" for both of her children. Later, and ideally, the recovery processes of all family members will merge.

Among the chief goals of therapy is to help these mothers identify and express all the losses they experience following the revelation of incest in the family. Helping them to put into words what they feel will help them to work through the complexities of grief. This in turn will help them to achieve a sense of resolution.

Powerlessness

The mother of a sexual abuse victim is likely to believe that she has seriously failed in her responsibilities as both a parent and a spouse. She is also likely to feel that events now control her life. She feels powerless. Individuals react to a sense of powerlessness in different ways. Some experience rage in an attempt to regain control. Apparent apathy or withdrawal can also be an expression of powerlessness; "I tried and I failed, I am not capable of looking after my child" is commonly heard.

Helping a mother discern the areas of life in which she does have power, and where she does not, will help her deal with the feelings of powerlessness. For example, while a mother's power in a child's life is limited, it is significant and can be used constructively. Acknowledging that she took action that resulted in the child being protected and cared for, once she knew about the abuse, can be a starting point for any mother to regain a feeling of being in control.

Including the mother in the treatment process is essential to reinforcing her sense of control and competence as a parent. Mothers, whenever possible, should be consulted and not "told" what action will be taken on behalf of their children. Providing information and guidance on what action in the child's recovery the mother can take is important. Resources should be provided as support to the mother (e.g., child care, financial assistance, legal counsel) and not as a replacement of her authority and responsibility in the family. I recommend against implementing any resource or support service without the agreement of the mother, unless it is essential to the child's safety or well-being.

In trying to compensate for a sense of powerlessness, a mother may believe that once her child is "cured," the perpetrator incarcerated, a new home is established, or a job started, then all is "normal." Any delays or disruptions to this goal of normalcy can be perceived as a failure on her part. A therapist needs to help the mother approach her tasks one step at a time. This will help her acknowledge her successes, focus her resources, and conserve her energy. Steady progress, even if limited, is better than radical changes. Radical changes have already been imposed on her and she needs time to deal with them.

Self-Esteem Issues

Many conditions affect a mother's level of self-esteem. Any risk or injury to her child will challenge her sense of competence and self-worth. Incest presents a very serious affront to her integrity as a mother.

Much of the literature has identified low self-esteem as a characteristic of the mothers of incest victims. It is not true, however, that the low self-esteem of a mother causes a child to be sexually abused. Unfortunately, emotional and psychological status, which include her self-esteem, are too often viewed as causing her husband's abuse of her child.

Self-esteem is a problem for parents in any context. Whatever a mother's previous sense of self worth, after her child has been abused it will likely be worse. Self-esteem is an indicator of one's psychological resources and feelings of competence. A lack of confidence in one's ability to perform as a parent can make even simple tasks seem overly complex. In my experience, the non-offending mother feels overwhelmed by the demands she believes are imposed on her. Fed by her perceived failure, she may feel paralyzed. Acknowledging her stress is important to her interpretation of her performance and ability. Giving a mother permission to be overwhelmed provides her with an opportunity to talk about what she is feeling. Acknowledging her successes can strengthen her self-esteem. Providing her with support and keeping expectations for her simple and short-term also will help.

6
THE NON-OFFENDING
MOTHER'S PERSONAL HISTORY

Unresolved problems from childhood can emerge when an individual is confronted with a serious emotional crises. If the unresolved problems are ignored, they function as unseen influences or inhibitors in the recovery process of both mother and child.

Successfully treating unresolved issues is difficult and time consuming. Initially, a mother may not want to undertake this exploration of her "inner world." However, a professional can assist in identifying emerging problems that are interfering with her ability to recover.

An in-depth exploration of a mother's experience is most effective once basic stability and security needs have been met (e.g., a new lifestyle is gaining familiarity, the child's well-being is more apparent, and the stage of

acceptance has remained stable for a period of time).
Exploring unresolved issues provides mothers with an
opportunity for personal growth. From the perspective
of the therapist, it is important not to allow the mother's
personal history to become confused as precipitating
factors in the sexual abuse of her child. However
traumatic the life experience of a non-offending mother,
or the character of that trauma, she needs to understand
that she did not consciously or unconsciously "cause" the
abuse.

As most therapists know, serious childhood trauma
impacts on an adult's self-esteem, world view,
expectations of self and others, and expectations of life
in general. In my experience with women who were
abused as children, their most common characteristic is
their belief that they cannot protect themselves from
adverse circumstances or relationships. Some even
believe that they deserve adversity. If they have no
boundaries for self-protection as individuals, they are
unlikely to have confidence in their ability to protect
their children. This does not mean that they do not *want*
to keep their children safe, happy and healthy. It may
mean they believe that they are incompetent to do so.

I have found it most effective to initially focus on the
fact that a mother has **survived** her own childhood
trauma. This draws her attention to potential and actual

strengths, and provides a real metaphor for her child's recovery. In my experience working with adult survivors of childhood trauma, rarely was there effective intervention in the traumatic event. Otherwise the issues or effects would not be presenting themselves as unresolved. This is a critical point for mothers of incest victims. These mothers have already introduced a significant change from their own childhood experience and from that of their children — they listened and they acted once they learned of the abuse.

In one family, the daughter disclosed the incest when in her mid-thirties. Her mother, a victim five decades earlier, had not known her child was sexually abused but had acquiesced to her husband's dominance and aggression because of her own low self-esteem and perceived powerlessness. Reminded that there were not the support services or general acknowledgement of sexual abuse when she was a child or young mother of six, she was able to see that by believing her daughter and by confronting her husband **now**, she was taking important steps forward from her own experience. The daughter, formerly convinced that her mother had refused to act as her protector, was able to see the love and caring in her mother's present actions.

The primary importance of unresolved issues for mothers is in the coping strategies they used to survive dangerous or painful events. A woman who learned to withdraw and to avoid an abusive confrontation with her parents, will need a more assertive strategy to deal with an angry offender or child. Violence tends to breed violence. A mother who was physically abused as a child may, under stress, become similarly abusive in response to her own child's anger or acting out. Understanding that hers is a learned response, and not an indication of a desire to harm her child, a mother is most able to use other strategies for dealing with her anger or distress.

A mother's past experience also make possible important moments of empathy with her children. She can empathize with their pain, their appreciation of adult support and intervention, and with their strength to survive successfully.

Non-offending mothers are not likely to seek help for resolving their childhood traumas until there is an external reason for doing so. This is due, at least in part, to a lingering belief that they were responsible for the abuse experienced in their childhood. If they experience family problems as adults, they may feel that this is only what they deserve. Helping them see that their unresolved problems are impeding their ability to care for their children may be the most effective means of engaging them in therapy. I have worked with several mothers and daughters who were sexually abused as children. When these mothers work through their own problems, this facilitates their openness, empathy and sharing of experiences. One of the most painful consequences for an incest victim is the perceived or actual isolation. If a mother and child can reduce this for one another, it is indeed a gift for both.

On the other hand, a woman who has not experienced any painful challenges will not automatically have more confidence in dealing with her child's sexual abuse than someone who is more "street wise." The woman whose experience conforms more to societal norms and expectations may be less prepared than a woman who has had more negative life experiences. She may feel more betrayed by life than someone who has already dealt with betrayal. She may feel a more radical shift in her self-image as a "good" mother and person. If she held the belief that "only bad things happen to bad people," she may now become a victim of her own biases. She may even be more resistant to support because she feels that she has much more to lose. It may be easier to deal with life crises when you expect them than if you believe they will never happen to *you*.

7

ISSUES IN PARENTING

Incest produces a crisis in a mother's relationship with her child. Changes and choices are forced upon each. Mothers need to recognize these changes, understand their origins, and make choices about what is desired. For some mothers, there occurs a subtle dependence on her child to resolve her turmoil (e.g., if her child becomes "happy," she will think that she too can be "happy;" if her child's nightmares stop, she too can sleep peacefully; and so on). This dependence needs to be addressed in the context of therapy.

The Child's Safety

The first priority of a non-offending mother is usually her child's protection from the offender. She will want to know that the offender will no longer have inappropriate access to the child. The complexity of the mother's concern in father/daughter incest should be acknowledged by those who seek to help her. A woman who has to leave her home to protect her child, or force her husband to do so, may need support in making decisions and accessing resources.

It is important not to interpret a mother's initial hesitation as not wanting to protect her child. Once she has made the decision to protect her child, she may be faced with having to provide for her child alone. If the necessary resources are available to her, and we empathize with the difficulty of her decision, we are likely to discover that she shares our goal of wanting what is best for her child.

A mother may press to have the offender arrested and as a result, be impatient with legal processes. She may seem antagonistic toward police officers or investigations. Focusing on what is being done to protect her child, and empathizing with her frustration, can help allay this stress.

Most mothers will appreciate support in following through with actions necessary to assure the child's safety. Simply handing them a list of phone numbers for agencies and professionals is unlikely to help.

The Child's Recovery Process

Once the child is safe, the mother will want to know the short- and long-term effects of the sexual abuse. Common questions from non-offending women will concern their children's sexual development, the impact on their current and future relationships with adults and other children, and the duration of current symptoms of stress (e.g., bedwetting, nightmares, aggressive acting out). It is doubtful that reassurance that everything will become "alright" is helpful; we cannot promise that the abuse will not result in some emotional scarring or social difficulties.

I have heard the following questions and comments from a number of mothers of sexually abused children:

- "Will she remember; what will she remember?"

- "What should I do when he says he hates his dad, or me?"

- "Will she have more problems when she's a teenager? Will it keep coming up again and again?"

- "What should I tell my other children? My friends? My family?"

- "Will the anger and nightmares ever stop?"

- "I'm so afraid to leave them with somebody. What should I do?"

- "How do you know this will help my child or me?"

- "Will I ever forget and trust anyone again?"

- "What did I do wrong?"

With most of these, honesty and simplicity are the most constructive strategies for concerned professionals. Sexual abuse is a life experience that is integrated; it doesn't just go away.   Like other life challenges, individuals can emerge stronger and wiser but with less innocence or naivete.   As professionals, parents or victims, we can only do the best we can with what we know at the time.   After twenty years experience with children and families in crisis, I do believe we are making progress in our response to childhood trauma. As healers we can offer the most important messages — compassion, courage and support.

We are learning that early intervention with sexually abused children can reduce much of their stress and reduce the negative effects that would otherwise be expected to occur. Mothers can be provided with information about their child's recovery stages and should be advised of the purpose of any intervention. Parents need to understand that what their child is experiencing at the moment will not necessarily be there forever.

I have encountered mothers who believe that the severity of the punishment the offender receives will proportionately reduce the severity of the negative consequences for her child. We should remind these mothers that the child's needs are most important, and that her child's recovery is not dependent on punishment of the offender. The mother needs to know that there are treatment programs which include the offender in the therapeutic process, but this is not always possible or desirable.

There is still much debate about children's rights and responsibilities in the courts. Parents will have to evaluate these rights and responsibilities. Again, we should empathize with their frustration and then help them focus on the constructive alternatives that are available.

In Canada and the United States there are sexual abuse treatment programs that include the offender in the treatment process. This approach should be carefully assessed by responsible professionals in cooperation with victims and non-offending parents before it is tried. Such an approach should not be forced on parent or child without their agreement. In addition to violating individual rights, the potential effectiveness of the treatment would be severely inhibited.

On the other hand, if it is the family's wish to have the offender remain in the home or involved with the family, an integrated and intense family therapy program is essential. The problems and issues precipitating the incest must be addressed, monitored and resolved for any confidence in the child's safety and security to be realistic.

Non-offending mothers are parenting children in pain. This will be manifested in a variety of ways, not always easy to deal with or accept. Non-offending mothers need information on the "normal" acting out following trauma. Assistance in child care, and opportunities to share their stress and frustration, can be helpful. Normal developmental needs and struggles of children are affected and can become distorted (i.e., with every problem being attributed to the sexual abuse, an idealized image of who the child "would have been" can emerge). Siblings will be affected and will increase demands on the parent. Whatever support acknowledges the stress, and makes efforts to relieve it in a manner meaningful to that mother, will be helpful.

Mothers will seek advice and support in how to respond or deal with their other children (e.g., "What do I tell them?"; "What do I do when they blame me for their daddy going away?"; "How do I explain to a six year old why his daddy might go to jail?"; "They don't know what to say to their freinds; what do I do?"). Once again there are no simple answers. My rule of thumb is honesty and openess; children make up what they don't understand and they are especially vulnerable to the gossip or interpretations of others outside the immediate family.

Mothers need, and deserve, all the support they can get in responding to the needs of their families. Friends and professionals can reinforce a mother's explanations and actions in their interactions with her children. Family therapy should involve siblings as well as the victimized child. Professionals must be sensitive and responsive to the needs and issues of children not involved in the incest directly, and offer them support. Like the non-offending mother, siblings are secondary victims. Included in the healing or recovery process, they will also share her status as a survivor.

Frequently one child's disclosure of incest opens the door for siblings to come forward. This can increase the mother's and the family's distress exponentially. It also offers the opportunity to resolve the problem once and for all. As with the parent-child relationship, a multiple disclosure can offer a family alienated by secrecy and shame to come together in empathy and compassion, with *new* family rules and dynamics.

Following the disclosure of incest, a non-offending mother's parenting skills and competence come under scrutiny. Past parenting strategies may no longer be effective or desirable. New approaches may not work immediately; they require time for both mother and child to adjust. The problems experienced will not always be simplistic instances of "behavior management," and will require a deeper understanding and evaluation of parenting approaches.

In incest, the court may order access to the offender. Usually this is "supervised access," where an objective third party monitors visits between the offender and the child. The non-offending parent will have to deal with her reactions to this and to the reactions of her child. Until the child adjusts to the new circumstances, she or he can be on an emotional rollercoaster before and after the visits. Both the non-offending parent and the child have to let go of their former relationship with the offender, even though he is still present in their lives. One task of the therapist is to assist family members in forging new and healthier relationships with each other following disclosure of incest.

A very difficult aspect for non-offending mothers to deal with is their child's anger, and that of siblings. Child victims will have ambiguous feelings about the offender. While they may have been afraid and disliked the sexual contact from the outset, there will have been dependence and usually affection for the offender in other contexts. The threat from the offender that maintained the child's secrecy may have been that the mother would become very angry and the family would be destroyed.

From the child victim's perspective, a non-offending mother's removing the children from the home or forcing the father to leave will be a fulfillment of that prophesy. In this confusion and pain, the child may project anger onto the mother, especially if the incestuous father has presented himself as a victim of circumstances. In the non-offending mother's decisions and actions following disclosure of the abuse, the child will again feel powerless, further fueling anger toward the mother.

The mother is likely to feel she is being challenged "on all fronts" when this anger is expressed. In her own stress and frustration, she may retaliate "in kind," only to chastise herself even more severely after the fact. She may expect the child to understand that she is protecting and caring for the family, forgetting that the child's own pain and feelings for the offender have emotional rather than rational or logical origins. Preparing the non-offending mother for her child's anger can assist her in not taking it as a personal attack. Her awareness of her own ambiguous feelings toward the offender can help her understand those of her child(ren). Both mother and child will benefit from having an alternate outlet, apart from the immediate family, to express thoughts and feelings.

My suggestion to parents in dealing with the child's anger is adaptable to both parent and child. Simply stated, guide them to express their feelings openly and in a manner that is not abusive to themselves or anyone else. For example, tell them that yelling is okay but calling people names or hitting them is not. If they must hit something, make sure it doesn't have feelings. If they don't want to talk yet, tell them that's okay and you will wait until they are ready. Tell them it's okay to be afraid, *and* not everything or everyone will try to hurt them. An angry child's feelings can be validated without harming another.

Support groups with parents in similar circumstances can be especially helpful. Sharing experiences with others can "normalize" the complex responses to the incest experience. Suggestions can be offered that have some basis with children in similar circumstances. A consistent opportunity to "unload" can offer a break from parenting and reduce the stress for the children as well. Twenty-four hour hot lines provide valuable support for parents comfortable with this kind of contact. Again, realizing the dynamics and finding constructive, appropriate alternatives is the goal. Role-inversion is often identified in incestuous families, with children assuming the functions and responsibilities of adults in the families. This too can be dealt with or prevented if the parent has positive adult support.

8
MOTHERS ARE PEOPLE TOO

The non-offending mothers of child sexual abuse victims face a challenge that every parent would dread. In incest, they confront a serious crime committed against their child by someone with whom they had a trusting relationship. A mother's temptation to deny that reality is not difficult to understand. It is also easy to understand that she will be angry with herself, the offender, her child and life itself.

Non-offending mothers might bargain with God, or whoever else might listen to them, to remove their pain and bring life back to normal. However, acceptance of the cards life has dealt them is the point where most of them will be able to take the next step.

The grief cycle of the non-offending mother is a natural response to a painful trauma. This grief cycle that is imposed on them means that they too are victims of incest.

These mothers deserve compassion and respect. I have not agreed with every decision a mother has made and, on occasion, I have had to intervene when I thought a child was at risk. However, this did not negate my belief that a mother was doing the best she could, given her resources and circumstances. This belief held the door open for both of us to receive information and to accommodate changing perceptions. In most cases we were able to take advantage of that opportunity.

The woman who returns to an offending spouse (whose promises of rehabilitation I, personally, do not trust), or who blames her child for the family's crisis, presents the most powerful challenge to my patience and values. I have found that I can disagree, and do what I deem necessary for the welfare of the child(ren), and at the same time have some understanding of the fears and issues motivating their mother. This understanding facilitates keeping the door open for further contact with mothers.

It is the inclination of children to love their parents. We, as professionals and parents, can protect and care for them without using hatred or criticism as the vehicle.

It is important to remember that the non-offending parent of a sexually abused child is not necessarily incompetent or inadequate, nor has she committed a crime. The goal is to help these parents work through their pain, and reconnect with their sense of personal power and self-esteem. It is then that they can *continue* to do the best they can for themselves and their children.

Bibliography

1. Bagley, Christopher and Margaret McDonald: *Adult Mental Health Sequels of Child Sexual Abuse, Physical Abuse, and Neglect in Maternally Separated Children;* Faculty of Social Welfare, University of Calgary and Department of Sociology, University of Surrey, England: October, 1984.

2. Bagley, Christopher and Richard Ramsay: *Disrupted Childhood and Vulnerability to Sexual Assault: Long Term Sequels With Implications for Counselling*; Faculty of Social Welfare, University of Calgary: February, 1985.

3. Belohlavek, Nancy and Geraldine Faria: "Treating Female Adult Survivors of Childhood Incest;" *Social Casework*, October, 1984.

4. Buck, Craig and Susan Forward: *Betrayal of Innocence: Incest and Devastation*; Penguin Books; England: 1984.

5. Burgess, Ann Wolbert: *Sexual Abuse of Children and Adolescents*; Lexington Books; Lexington, Mass.: 1978.

6. Butler, Sandra: *Conspiracy of Silence: The Trauma of Incest*; Volcano Press Inc.; San Francisco: 1978.

7. Cohn, Ann H.: *An Approach to Preventing Child Abuse*; National Committee for the Prevention of Child Abuse; Washington, D.C.: 1984.

8. Dietz, Christine A. and Croft John L.: "Family Dynamics of Incest: A New Perspective;" *Social Casework*, 1980; Family Services Association of America: Pages 602-8.

9. Delin, Bart: *The Sex Offender*; Beacon Press; Boston: 1978.

10. deYoung, Mary: *The Sexual Victimization of Children*; McFarland and Company Inc.: Jefferson, N.C.: 1982.

11. Gauzer, Marion: *Sexuality Concerns of Sexual Assault Survivors*; Calgary Sexual Assault Centre; Calgary: 1985.

12. Geiser, Robert L.: *Hidden Victims: The Sexual Abuse of Children*; Beacon Press; Boston: 1979.

13. Groth, Nicholas A.: *Men Who Rape: The Psychology of the Offender*; Plenum Press; New York: 1979.

14. Helfer, Ray E. and C. Henry Kempe: *The Battered Child*; University of Chicago Press; Chicago: 1974.

15. Herman, Judith Lewis and Lisa Hirschman: *Father-Daughter Incest*; Harvard University Press; Cambridge, Massachusetts: 1981.

16. Holder, Wayne M. and Patricia Schnene: *Understanding Child Neglect and Abuse*; American Humane Association; Denver, Colorado: 1981.

17. Kaplan-Sanoff, Margot and Esther Finc-Kletter: "The Developmental Needs of Abused Children"; *Beginnings*; Redmond, Washington: Fall, 1985.

18. Kempe, C. Henry and Ruth S. Kempe: *The Common Secret: Sexual Abuse of Children and Adolescents*; W.H. Freeman and Company, New York: 1984.

19. Lawton-Speert, Sarah and Andy Wachtel: *Child Sexual Abuse in the Family*; Social Planning and Research, United Way of the Lower Mainland; Vancouver, B.C.: 1982.

20. London Rape Crisis Centre: *Sexual Violence: The Reality for Women*; Women's Press; London: 1984.

21. McIntyre, Kevin, MSSW: "Role of Mothers in Father-Daughter Incest: A Feminist Analysis;" *Social Work*, November, 1980; National Association of Social Workers Inc.: Pages 462-6.

22. Nanaimo Rape Assault Centre: *Realities of Child Sexual Abuse*; Nanaimo, B.C.: 1983.

23. Porter, Ruther (Editor): *Child Sexual Abuse Within the Family*; Travistock Publications; New York: 1984.

24. Sanford, Linda Tscherhart: *The Silent Children*; McGraw-Hill; New York: 1984.

25. Schultz, Le Roy G. (Editor): *The Sexual Victimology of Youth*; Charles C. Thomas Publisher; Springfield, Illinois: 1980.

26. Summit, Roland M.D. and JoAnn Kryso M.S.W.: "Sexual Abuse of Children;" American Journal of Orthopsychiatry: April, 1973.

Recommended Readings

Incest

Allen, Charlotte. *Daddy's Girl*. Wyndham Books, Toronto, 1980.

Armstrong, Louise. *Kiss Daddy Goodnight*. Hawthorne Books, New York, NY, 1978.

Brady, Katherine. *Father's Days*. Seaview Books, New York, NY, 1979.

Butler, Sandra. *Conspiracy of Silence*. New Glide Publications, San Francisco, CA, 1978.

Herman, Judith. *Father-Daughter Incest*. Harvard Press, Cambridge, MA, 1981.

Justice, Blair. *Broken Taboo*. Human Science Press, New York, NY, 1978.

Renvoize, Jean. *Incest - A Family Pattern*. Rutlege & Kegan Hall, 1982.

Sandford, Linda. *The Silent Children*. Anchor Press, New York, NY, 1980.

Child Sexual Abuse

Adams, C. and Fay, J. *No More Secrets*. Impact Publishers, USA, 1981.

Burgess, A. et al. *Sexual Assault of Children and Adolescents*. Lexington Books, Lexington, MA, 1978.

Bush, Florence. *The Best Kept Secret*. Prentice Hall, NJ, 1980.

Carver County Program. *Children Need Protection*. USA, 1980.

Geiser, Robert. *Hidden Victims*. Beacon Press, Boston, MA, 1979.

Inglis, Ruth. *Sins of the Father*. Peter Owen, London, 1978.

Lindendecker, Cliff. *Children in Crisis*. Everest House, New York, NY, 1981.

Willick, Ray. *The Troubled Ones*. Hill of Content, New York, NY, 1979.

Clinical

Briere, John. *Beyond Survival* (forthcoming).

Byerly, Carolyn. *The Mother's Book: How to Survive the Incest of Your Child.* Kendall/Hunt Publishing, Dubuque, IA, 1985.

Courtois, Christine. *Healing the Incest Wound.* Norton, New York, 1988.

Faller, K.C. *Child Sexual Abuse: An Interdisciplinary Manual for Diagnosis, Case Management and Treatment.* Columbia University Press, New York, 1988.

Herman, Judith. *Father-Daughter Incest.* Harvard University Press, Cambridge, MA, 1981.

Maltz, Wendy and Beverly Holman. *Incest and Sexuality: A Guide to Understanding and Healing.* Lexington Books, Lexington, MA, 1987.

Miller, Alice. *Thou Shalt Not Be Aware: Society's Betrayal of the Child.* New American Library, New York, 1986.

NiCarthy, Ginny, Karen Merriam, and Sandra Coffman. *Talking It Out: A Guide to Groups for Abused Women.* Seal Press, Seattle, WA, 1984.

Salter, Anna C. *Treating Child Sex Offenders.* Sage Publishing, Newbury Park, CA, 1988.

Walker, Lenore (ed.). *Handbook on Sexual Abuse of Children.* Springer, New York, 1988.

White, Evelyn C. *Chain Chain Change: For Black Women Dealing with Physical and Emotional Abuse.* New Leaf Series/Seal Press, Seattle, WA, 1984.

Self Help

Bass, Ellen and Louise Thornton (ed.). *Courage to Heal: A Guide for Women Survivors of Child Sexual Abuse.* Harper and Row, New York, 1988.

Treating Abused Adolescents

A Program for Providing Individual and Group Therapy

Darlene Anderson Merchant

TREATMENT IS THE FOCUS in this new book for therapists who work with adolescent victims of multiple abuse. Its techniques emerge from the orientation that therapies must, where possible, address the entire family. Homes in which abuse occurs—even if an outsider has inflicted it—are often dysfunctional; emotional neglect, shaming, and poor parenting may underlie the victimization. Correcting these problems can produce both a deeper recovery and better protection against future episodes.

This program aids in treating the spectrum of physical, neglectful and sexual abuse. Youths aged 12-18 are the focus, though many therapies apply equally to younger children. These recommendations may also be applied for victims whose families cannot or will not become involved.

Field development of this program occurred at the Adolescent Victim Counseling Project, Storefront/Youth Action of Richfield, Minnesota.

CONTENTS: Identifying Abuse: Depression, low self-esteem and unhealthy relationships, aggression, emotional-physical-sexual abuse • Family Dynamics: multi-generational abuse, enmeshment-disengagement patterns, shame patterns, the use of power roles, role reversals and removal of boundaries, parenting, life changes • Responsibility in Therapy: Offending parents, non-offending parents, non-abused siblings, conflict between parents, family communications, parenting techniques • Non-intact family therapy: Treatment for adolescents: an abuse protocol, talking about abuse, reporting, individual therapy, group therapy • Other needs: Self-esteem, trust, intimacy, sexuality, overcoming victim role-playing, overcoming grief • Entering therapy: uncovering abuse; information parents need, the first session, advantageous peer or family sessions • Interrelated needs or complications: substance abuse, physical problems, suicide.

Cat. #177, ISBN 1-55691-017-7

Child Sexual Abuse And the Courts

A Manual for Therapists

Adele Mayer

EACH YEAR SEES an increase in sexual abuse cases heard in criminal courts, and many jurisdictions now have special units devoted to them. Child victims are testifying routinely. Behavioral health specialists are also being subpoenaed as expert witnesses.

This manual addresses the roles of both the therapist and victim in every aspect of the proceedings. Topics range from case preparation through coordination with other court parties, and actual testimony. Therapists and victims alike will find this briefing indispensable.

Indeed, in the process of recovery and therapy the adjudication process looms large. Seeing justice prevail may bring closure to painful resentments—a healthy vindication. On the other hand, a rough cross-examination or unexpected reversals can redouble the client's trauma—not to mention the therapist's—and compound the later challenge of healing.

Child victims especially must understand each legal step. Many of the exercises here can be used with, or modified for, children of any age. The focus is on intrafamilial molestation, since the complications of these cases exert a powerful effect on child victims in court.

Contents: Testimony (by therapist and victim) ● Complete preparation and procedures ● Ethical considerations ● Common defense tactics ● Coping with stress ● Court preparation: decisions about testifying, preparation, affirmations; the okay script, recommendations ● Special situations: daycare, mentally handicapped, male victims, mother-daughter ● Plea bargains, recantations; heresay / excited utterance; videotaping ● Assertiveness ● Issues of credibility, fabrication, competence ● Parental attitudes ● Serving as an expert witness ● Appendices, Bibliographies, References, Index.

Cat. #460 ISBN 1-55691-046-0 Softcover